Maryam K. Muhammad

WHY......

I AM ENOUGH

Why I Am Enough

All rights reserved
ISBN: 978-1-936937-44-8

Published in the United States of America

First Edition

Book Layout By
RATHSI Publishing, LLC
rathsipublishing@gmail.com

No part of this book may be used or reproduced in any manner whatsoever without written permission except in the case of brief quotations embodied in critical articles and reviews.

For information address:
www.HTLC19.com
All Social Media @HTLC19

Introduction

It was about January or February of 2017 when my sister and friend, Maryam K. Muhammad told me about a vision for a book that she wanted to write. This book was to be a testament to the special relationship, lessons, and insights that she received from her grandmother, Sis. Burnsteen Muhammad, one of the pioneers of the Nation of Islam. The connection between the two was always on the forefront of Maryam's mind and heart; it was something she questioned, at times rejected, but at one point - it became that "thing" she could no longer ignore.

As an outsider quietly observing her on the journey of drawing on lessons from her grandmother, I knew there was one thing I could be certain of - both women had an intense passion and concern for women all over the planet and their spiritual well being. The connection and awareness of God and "spirit" in all of our affairs was not something that Maryam could separate from her work with women. And from her own reflection, she felt that her personal interests in spiritual matters was in fact, a continuation of the work her grandmother, who was affectionately known as "Reformer".

Although it has been many years since the transition of Sis. Burnsteen, her impact has been evident in Maryam's life and continues to reveal itself everyday. Needless to say, it is now 2018 and Maryam Muhammad has finally finished THIS work. And just in case you hadn't noticed, it does not hold insight into her grandmother and their relationship, per se. In fact, it is NOT the book we talked about last year at all! What it is and what it does, is explore some of the guiding principles and the exploration of self that began years ago as Maryam began exploring the significance of her ancestor's work and her own personal mission.

In this book, you will find a variety of topics, reflections, and even activities. They are written with transparency and authenticity on the part of the writer. What you see are insights from her mind that are a result of her personal life experiences, but also a response to many of the women and girls she's worked with over the years. As I looked over the final collection of writings, I felt both reflective and inspired. I saw a glimpse of God and I saw a glimpse of myself. I also felt a deep connection to women all over the planet that have dealt with some of what is addressed here: the poor choices, negativity, lack of vision, abuse, pain, etc. I also felt connected to the victories and sense of empowerment in the inspired words of the author. To me, it felt...real.

As you engage this book, be open to the experience of a human being: a human being vulnerable; a human being accepted; a human being afraid; a human being courageous, and most importantly, a human being connected to God! What better comfort is that?!?

May God allow you to receive what He has in store for you through the words of the author, Maryam Muhammad. Let this be the beginning of a new world that begins with the mind and hearts of women who are directly and intentionally connected to their Creator!

With love,

Sis. Mareshah Muhammad

Author's Preface

In writing this book I have cried, screamed, thanked God, laughed and meditated. I have felt release from my inner pain and I'm praying that many of God's women who read this book feel a form of release as well. We are all God's girls looking for Him to restore us in one way or another. My personal proof and testimony is my grandmother. She is my inspiration and my strength. She lives both through me and in many of the words written in this book.

My grandmother, Sis. Burnsteen Muhammad, was given an envelope by God. An envelope symbolizes a covering. It completely surrounds and protects the message held inside. She was told to never leave home without it until she was to see God again. As God's girls, He covers and protects us as long as we put on His armor. We must cloak ourselves with the essence of God. We are carriers of His message. All human life born comes through the vessel of a female. We carry the answers to man's prayers and the evidence of how God created Himself.

While writing this book I often thought of one of my favorite biblical women, Mary of Magdalene. She was ostracized by her own community, yet Jesus still saw her, reformed her, and made her his messenger to carry the message of his resurrection. No matter what condition we come to God in, He accepts us. Regardless to how this world stereotypes and befouls us, He still accepts us. He cleanses us by showering us with His love and truth. Mary of Magdalene used expensive oil to clean Jesus's feet. It has been stated by scholars that the oil she used was lavender – a well-known oil used today. Most of us don't even know its history nor its healing powers. I used to ask myself, did she ever reach a point in her life where she cleansed herself with the same oil? Because she learned she was just as valuable in the eyes of God.

I pray that the words in this book restore and strengthen our faith and inspire belief. And serve as a reminder that we should go **nowhere** without putting on the full armor of God.

You are like a rose!

A rose represents love, perfection, beauty, renewal and the triumph of the spirit over matter as the rose bursts open……out of a muddy earth.

Red roses mean passion and sacrifice.

The love that a rose symbolizes continues to survive regardless to its surroundings.

The pedals of a rose form a perfectly symmetrical circle around a yellow center, which is evocative of the sun.

Roses symbolize the heart, life & life's mystery.

Roses have powerful energy fields that vibrate at a high electrical frequency. It is the highest of any other flower on the earth.

Muslims view roses as symbols of the human soul, so smelling the scent of a rose reminds them of their own spirituality.

Mary, the mother of Jesus is referred to as the thornless rose. Because she knew her protection came from within not from without.

"God has made you, everything that you need to be to exist in this life God has already put it inside of you. But you have to become aware of what God has done for you. And then with a proper relationship with Him you begin to unfold. " The Hon. Min. Louis Farrakhan

Contents

Dear Sisters	14
The Journey of Faith	26
Creating a Healthy Mindset	36
Excuses…Why Use Them?	48
Overcoming the Difficulties Life May Bring	62
My Sisters Prayers…Silently Releasing the Pain That Haunts Me	78
Affirming Myself to a New Way of Living	92
Goal Setting	120
Acknowledgements	124

Dear Sisters

Sisters, we are creators. We manifest realities. We are builders of civilizations - the backbone of our villages and mothers of this universe.

We are fighters, warriors, God's soldiers! We leap over obstacles and break down barriers.

We create songs for survival. We move strategically with masterful rhythm. We are unstoppable!

The answers to man's prayers come through our womb. To mistreat a woman is like committing suicide on yourself. We are walking blessings sent from God.

Sisters, the relationship God has with us is an example of the type of relationship we should have with a man.

God loves me more than I love Him.
God lifts me & keeps me in my natural place.
God provides for me without complaining.
God opens doors for me.
God respects me.
God protects me.
God is merciful, patient, understanding of my pain and my redeemer.

It is important to find a man who is awakened to the God within himself and connected to the Creator of self. Learn your power to nurture and bring out that God in him if he's worth your gift. Know your value in the eyes of God!

Pray and God will lead you!

To my sisters,

I wasn't born with wings. My steps were out of faith. I couldn't see my road. I didn't know my guide. I only had faith and some days I only had fear. I never really had support.

Instead of being born with wings, I was born with opposition as my companion. Love was always a challenge accompanied by pain. My tears became the water that feeds my soul.

I was not born with wings, but there was a moving force within me. Its vibration I couldn't ignore. I was reminded of it every morning when I stared at God's mirroring image in my reflection.

No, I was not born with wings. Instead I was born with the ability to believe in the unseen - knowing when I fall I would get back up. You don't need wings when you're connected to the force of God's will. His will. That lifts, guides and moves you in the direction He has destined for you.

Learn to fly with your Creator and you won't need wings.

Sisters,

We all seek a peace of mind. But sometimes, we're not courageous enough to go and get it.

We hesitate when it comes to developing our greatness but we run to foolishness. We spend money on everything except on that which will make us better.

We allow others to pull us down.

STOP! At this moment, STOP doubting yourself. STOP caring what others may think. STOP thinking less of yourself.

You are more. You are powerful. You are a direct descendant of God. The Universe is here to serve you. Call on it with conviction and watch your reality change.

Sisters,

We hear and we obey the voice of God! His energy can be sent through any vessel He chooses.

His energy…His Essence is in you!

Don't let anyone interfere with your intimate relationship with God. He's calling us and we MUST be obedient to that call.

Do you want to let go of the pain you have inside? Remove doubt and insecurities? Be comforted in the arms of God?

We don't have to falsify our appearance with Him. Come to Him as you are and receive your healing!

A woman's heart should be so deep in God that a man would have to seek God to find it!

Nature is a powerful feminine force!

There is no reason why any woman should be standing still!

It is key to surround yourself with positive people who have goals in life that they are reaching. People who know what it's like to succeed in life. People who know what it's like to fall and get back up. They are overcoming the difficulties most people give up on. You want to surround yourself with people who carry the mindset you're looking to gain. People who are humble yet convicted in what they believe in. Those that exemplify strength and show genuine love in helping others.

Surround yourself with winners. People who keep up healthy conversations that produce progress - not those who only want to gossip about someone's shortcomings or complain about where they are in life and how they're not going anywhere.

Always remember positive energy will push you forward allowing you to fly free. Negative energy will only weigh you down.

Dear Sisters,

Communication is key!

We are, by nature, social beings. We must communicate with others in order to maintain a healthy mental state. But, that healthy mental state relies on what you are communicating. Is it positive or negative? Because we are social beings, we are drawn to communication - whether the substance is communicating to us or we are communicating to it. Therefore, we have to become disciplined in the law of attraction. What you put out is what you will get back. If you put out positive energy, you'll get back positive energy. If you put out negative energy, you'll get back negative energy.

Don't feed yourself destruction.

Dear Sisters,

Stop chasing your pain. You will never be good enough for a man who doesn't value your worth. Who doesn't respect you, honor you, take time to understand you or create a secure place for you in the future!

Chasing him feeds his ego and your pain, depleting your self-esteem while building his.

Love yourself enough to know you are worth more. Love God enough to know He created you to receive more!

Say goodbye to pain and open the door to happiness. You deserve it!

The Journey of Faith

Footsteps to faith,

Walking life's journey isn't an easy task, but it's a mission you were born equipped to win. Someone told you that when you see one set of footprints in your life's journey that means God didn't leave you, but He was carrying you.

I say that one set of footprints is when we became one with our Creator. We submitted to His will, we became obedient to His desires, and we allowed the God in us to be awakened and rise to its purpose.

Walk with the power of God. Have faith that moves mountains and receive the rewards on the other side.

Faith conquers fear. How do you move barriers? How do you overcome difficulties? How do you rise from your falls?

Answer- By building faith in the unseen. By strengthening your relationship with your Creator. Faith has five letters. The number five means power and it symbolizes God's grace. Connect with the God in you and see how powerful you become.

No matter what type of trial you may be experiencing, don't let go of the only one who has the power to see you through it. Become one with your Creator.

Faith is the key that will free you from your burdens. Faith is the seed worthy of planting into your soul. Nurture that seed with belief, water it with truth, and secure it with obedience to God.

Faith isn't always easy. Sometimes it's a challenging struggle, an internal tug of war.

You have to stay focused and believe in the unseen. Yes it is painful, but if you hold on, the blessing is always rewarding.

Turn fear into faith & watch it become the fuel of your existence!

Put on your armor of God. He is your protection. When our tears produce the rain, He is our umbrella. When our volcanic anger erupts and creates lava, He takes the lava and creates islands displaying beauty and peace.

When we are attacked by outside or inside forces, God produces the force field that cannot be penetrated. When pain hits us like our souls have been knocked out of our bodies; He grabs us, heals us, restores us, secures us, regenerates us all out of the pure love He has for us.

We are His soldiers conquering battles and winning wars. Let us give God our entire being in prayer, so that we remain protected.

Walking out on faith requires courage.

Patience strengthens faith, builds trust, and removes doubt.

Creating a Healthy Mindset

You are not a mistake! God created you on purpose. Claim your existence! You are a gift to this world. Move with the power of this Universe.

Stimulate your mind and your soul with the words of God. Stay focused on Him Who has given you your purpose and watch your energy maximize.

Many of us have been hurt by men. So we now walk around with war wounds, scars from the battlefields of being. We've become bitter, deceitful, angry, resentful and dissatisfied with life. When we have yet to live.

We are jewels of God's treasure chest. Some of us may be dull. Some may even be broken. But it is through His Word that we become polished and mended. We are the best! We just have to strengthen our relationship with The One who is the key to our success. He is The Light in our darkness, The Water that quenches our thirst. He is The Food that nourishes our existence, The Oxygen that feeds our cells. He is our beginning and through Him we will have no end.

Strengthen your relationship with God! Only He has the power to bring us out of the bondage of self and into the freedom of Himself!

The anger that separates us from one another also divides us internally from ourselves. Mend your differences. Reach out to someone you haven't had the courage to tell "I'm sorry".

Take a deep breath. Inhale new life and exhale old things. Surround yourself with the color that brings you joy.

Laugh for healing......smile in harmony with your soul...... and become a regenerated vessel!

Pain accompanies growth. Discomfort is your friend not your enemy. It forces you to create movement. Just make sure that movement is forward not backwards.

No one wants to repeat the same pain! Learn from it the first time.

Learn the lesson so that you may be released from the trial.

Why house hate in our hearts for someone when God doesn't house hate in His heart for us, even when we are being disobedient to Him. Let's live by His example.

You were born on purpose with a purpose. God has a plan for you and it is time to seek it and achieve it.

Walk with God and no one else! His essence is in you. Pull on it and use it. Settle on God's energy from this day forward!

Claim your victory. You're already winning!

Focus and let "petty" go. Concentrate on making positive moments in your life and stop animating yourself with being "petty".

The characteristics of a stereotypical woman defined by others don't belong to you. Embrace the nature God has given you!

Excuses... Why Use Them?

Don't let excuses become your reality! Learn to identify the difference between an excuse and a reason.

For some, excuses have shaped and molded their lives. They have become building blocks leading to walls of resistance. It is important to understand what is the difference between an excuse and a reason. An excuse (according to Oxford Dictionary & Dictionary.com), means to seek to lessen the blame attaching to (a fault or offence); try to justify; overlook or make allowances for; to release from an obligation or duty. A quote that explains what an excuse is, that I personally love, "Excuses are monuments of nothingness, they build bridges to nowhere and those who use them are masters of incompetence." -Author Unknown

The definition of reason (according to Dictionary.com) is a cause, explanation, or justification for an action or event; the powers of the mind to think, understand, and form judgments by a process of logic. When we create a reason for something, it takes a process of logical thinking. An excuse is not logical. You actually have to have a reason before you give an excuse. So why not stop at the reason or follow the reason up with a coherent action and not an irrational one? Why do we go further and give excuses when the reason has already been determined?

Excuses can become hidden lies, creating false realities, making us weak and fearful individuals.

A reason gives the mind the power to think. It allows us to logically execute our thoughts. Giving the God in you the power to manifest itself and overpower the weaker side of self that would rather use an excuse.

The root of a lot of excuses is fear. Because you are afraid of a response, results, someone's opinion, etc. Fear is a distressing emotion. When distress is present in your mind, you will produce anxiety, mental suffering, pain, a sense of danger, and apprehension. All of these emotions cause you to create an excuse so you can quickly elevate your body from experiencing a temporary fright.

Stop creating pathways of irrational thinking when all you have to do is challenge the fear to produce logical thinking and create the ability to solve problems.

Stop creating excuses that give us false justifications to the activities that we indulge in everyday. That creates nonproductive behavior.

Some of us carry excuses in our DNA, because of fear of circumstances. For example: When the slave master would come and say our ancestors' son was smart or had gifts, we would use excuses to why he wasn't. We would say, "No sir Massa, you don't want him. He's nothing but trouble." We knew our children were gifted, but we needed to create an excuse for the survival of our families. Now, today we do the same thing not knowing why. As soon as someone compliments your child you come up with excuses as to why what he or she is saying about your child isn't true. When there is a side of you knowing the absolute truth, which is that your child is what the person stated. Or even when you are dealing with your own self. Why can't you accept compliments or believe you are more than your circumstances?

Fear and doubt overcome the truth inside and allows the excuse to manifest. Retrain your thoughts to challenge the fear and remove the doubt to change your wellbeing.

How we overcome excuses matures our state of mind.

To mature means you produce natural growth and development. Breaking a bad habit takes time. Give yourself 21 days to break the habit of excuse making. Putting yourself on a realistic timeframe will produce a natural change in your life that you can adapt to and maintain.

You didn't start mastering making excuses overnight; do not expect yourself to stop making them overnight. But always remember, whatever you put your mind to doing, you have the ability to get it done. Your desire will feed the force inside of you to manifest the motion that will bring whatever you are trying to do into a reality.

Maturing your thinking to a higher level eliminates the need to make excuses.

Cultivate your mind by removing doubt and fear.

Develop your thinking by feeding yourself positive thoughts, words of strength and encouragement.

Always remember doubt creates resistance that feeds fear, ultimately telling you that it's easier to make an excuse than a sensible response.

Don't be afraid to take responsibility for your actions or to create new things. Living a purpose-filled life calls for adventure, difficulties, pains, success and more. The more you learn to eliminate excuses, the more you will begin to live on purpose.

One of the easiest ways to eliminate excuses is to educate yourself on why you're making them.

We sometimes make excuses because we have a lack of resources, limited knowledge, or even because we don't believe in ourselves.

Tell yourself at this moment, "Excuse making MUST come to an end."

Believe in yourself. You are a seeker of knowledge by nature.

You WILL acquire the resources you need. Speak it into existence.

Focus on manifesting a positive reality that will not have a need to create excuses.

You can do it. You were made to accomplish greater things in life.

Overcoming the Difficulties Life May Bring

As I am in search for Adam,

The first to be created of man, I'm constantly reminded of snakes and Eve eating from the wrong tree. As I am in search for Adam, the one that should be God's design of the man He would desire for me, I find products like Cain, who was overcome with envy for his brother because Able was given attention that Cain thought he should receive.

In my search, I realized that I was searching for Adam thinking I was Eve. Thinking that I was the downfall to man. Thinking that I was the beginning to a woman's pain. But I found that my quest was wrong. It was being incorrectly guided. First, if you look in the book of Genesis, you'll see that Eve wasn't even created when God gave Adam the instruction not to eat from the wrong tree. Eve came later. This produced another thought in my mind.

If Eve was produced after the instruction was given, can Eve be a state of mind? Adam represented both man and woman. He carries the X and Y chromosome. Adam was tempted to eat from the wrong tree like a man tempted to taste another man's right hand possession. When Adam created the thought of disobedience, he manifested the action that brought the thought into a reality. This is what gave birth to Eve.

Eve is a condition of the mind, not a gender. Women are not the downfall of man or the beginning point to a woman's pain. Eve represents the setting of the sun, that's why we have what is called the evening, which is the opposite of the day. It is darkness, and women have lived in darkness for generations of time because we have a misunderstanding of Eve. But now, it is time to relieve and release our minds and allow the light of the truth to come in.

Women are the embodiment of God's creative force. We are His feminine attributes. We are His laboratories that He uses to recreate His original creation, which was Himself. We are not only from God. We belong to God!

Like the sun, we nurture His creation with the warmth of our hearts, the core of our being. But, we also have adopted the distance created between the sun and God's creation, so our flames don't burn them. But with the proper armor you, can be permitted to touch the sun.

Only let a man who comes wearing the armor of God penetrate your atmosphere. Only he can soothe your flames and indulge in your nature. Women, we MUST stop searching for the wrong Adam because we are not that Eve!

A meditating moment…

I saw my foolishness, my weaknesses, my insecurities, and my instabilities, but most importantly I saw myself causing me pain. I'm on a path from wounded to healing. Putting an end to year-after-year-after-year of unnecessary discomfort. From this day forth, I will shed the skin that was the darkness of my pain.

Today is a very important day for me. My emotions are all over the place and I am very nervous. So I decided to call out for the one I love. I first called out to him with my heart, but I got no response. I then sent a text message but I got no response.

I waited and hours passed. I sent another text and I got no response. Later on that night, I sent two more texts and still, NO response. Knowing how important this day was for me, I got no response… I GOT NO DAMN RESPONSE!

No matter what, I've always been there for him. Always walking in his shadow, supporting him, and being masked by his essence. Blending in with his reflection so perfectly I became a part of him. Because my love for him allowed me to be cloaked by what I thought were his fundamental qualities.

But when there was no response, my eyes opened and my heart began to close. My trust left and my suspicion rose. I stepped out of the shadow and into the light. I realized I am stepping out of the darkness of pain into the light and comfort of God's bosom! I will never be victimized again by, "No DAMN Response!"

Dreams come in an unconscious state of mind. Visions are seen when the mind is in an awakened state. Don't live life with hope or be dreamer that stands still. Be a visionary that creates motion and masters its connection to the force of the unseen.

Visions are greater than the goal.

An adulterous relationship…

I thank you for granting me a moment in time where I felt a covering, like a foundation, because you concealed my imperfections. You were my CPR compressions that produced a rhythm in my heart that didn't let my past and my future stand apart. My present was truly a gift.

And now I'm struggling as my emotions are forced to shift. Setting me straight, so I can no longer be bait but instead annihilate this false state of mind. So I can find or more so open up my eyes to the one I gave myself to. I've got to let go and stop thinking that was you.

I have to visualize my reality and stop thinking that it is you for eternity. I've got to let go of this flow inside of me because the current is drowning me drastically, suffocating me critically, taking my breath expeditiously. All because in the end, I thought it would be you and me.

I was ready to say, "I do". I was willing to extend your life; I wanted to be the best wife. I felt the love like Mary had for Joseph. The kind that transmitted itself through distance, it was persistent. Like Noah's obedience to build an ark, or Moses' strength to lead, or was it like the Eve side of Adam eating from the wrong tree? That compelled me to believe there was no one else for me.

I thought I felt chemistry. But our properties didn't react the same instead they created a flame. Producing degrees beyond recognition, leaving scaring beyond redemption. You let go of my destiny, you couldn't handle the royalties of this majesty, and majestically you were engulfed in your own stupidity, ignorantly living your life as a catastrophe. Causing others to indulge in your mentality, but me, I had to go free.

Like the winds in a hurricane, I had to gain back my turf, coming in tune with my worth. I am the earth…quake that caused us to separate. Yes, I said I am the earthquake that caused us to separate.

Fear may be present on this life's journey, but it will not influence my direction. God is my pilot, His Christ in my co-pilot, His Comfort and Divine Guidance is my flight attendant and my seat belt represents my obedience to His Will.

I am going to wait for God to text me back. He won't irritate my mind, or upset my soul, or have me tapping my feet wondering what's taking so long. And even if He responds to others before He texts me back, I know my text will be unique and designed from His perfected, intimate love that only He has for me.

God will never take advantage of me or mislead me or even play with my emotions. God will never cheat on me, damage me or defile me. So as I wait for Him to text me back, my patience will grow immaculately because in Him, I am free from the impurities and labels others have placed on me.

Ttyl cuz I'm waiting on God to text me back!

When your inner self awakens and removes insecurities and you strengthen your self-love, you will begin to recognize those around you who love to see you weak.

Why did I want to commit suicide?

Why did I decide to inflict pain on myself that others had inflicted on me? Why did I decide to end my precious life thinking that I would relieve others from my presence, but never thinking they didn't think that much of me to relieve me of theirs?

Why would I consider everyone's thoughts about me except the thoughts of the One who created me? The One that said, "I will blow my breath in this child who ultimately belongs to Me". The One who hurts when I don't turn to Him, especially in my time of need.

Suicide is a quick means to an end. It is the devil's trick to get rid of lives that have the potential of getting rid of his. Suicide cheats us out of our greatness. It robs us of our fame, it takes away our existence and in the end it rewards all of those who were against our endurance, continuance, perseverance and our newfound commitment to live in God's presence.

Count your blessings, not your problems. And remember what you think is a problem could be a blessing in disguise.

You can dream and you can vision. If it stays in your mind, it will never become a reality.

My Sisters Prayers....
Silently Releasing The
Pain That Haunts Me

What are we battling within that stops us from turning to God and praying? God said come to Him. No one, no object, or no experience has the power to change that instruction, but God.

Reject that which keeps you on a horizontal plane of existence. Only the dead are to stay in a horizontal position. When you rise to prayer, you rise to life. It allows us to be risen into Him who has created us.

A prayer manifested from life's experiences…

Dear God,

I know I have asked for growth in my life, but sometimes the pain of letting go of the old or what doesn't belong to me becomes unbearable. I feel like I am in a fallen state. I watch people who come in my life, leave. Sometimes the pain of loss feels like death. Can you please help me God?

Answer….
When you plant a seed in the earth, its roots go down deep to become grounded and firmly rooted before it rises to its breakthrough and begins to blossom. Your seed grew into the tree that represents many levels of life. Your branches are roads God ordained you to take and your leaves are the people you've come in contact with.

In some seasons, the leaves stay and in others, they leave. But your branches will never break. They will only be pruned. Your trunk is strong because it's connected to the roots of God. Everyone is not made to approve, understand or accept your purpose in life but don't let that stop you from living it. When your tree undergoes death to produce more life, it is in its most beautiful state. It manifests the various hues of life.

Pain is the prerequisite of growth. When it begins to feel unbearable assess your life. See if you placed something or allowed someone else to place something in your path that doesn't belong. Because what God gives will never feel unnatural.

Rise every morning to prayer and thank God for everything He permits you to experience in life. He created you strong enough to get through it.

Dear God,

Give your women the strength to straighten up their backs and walk with their heads risen feeling your rhythm flowing through them. Let them know life's storms will come. But you possess the power to stop the winds from blowing, the ground from shaking and the rain from pouring. Equip my sisters to start their day with what they need to defeat everything that will come their way trying to break them down. Eliminate the element of surprise by providing us with the understanding that proper preparation starts with our relationship with You.

My sisters, winds will blow, seasons will change, but the warmth of God will always be present. Rise every morning and connect with Him.

Dear God,

Bless us to believe in the truth of Your existence. It's not easy to believe in something you cannot see nor touch, but are told is there. Yet, we don't have an issue believing the air we breathe exists, considering that we cannot see it. We believe we have a soul, but have never seen one. Why is it that we believe in those things, but when it comes to You, we have questions and doubt?

Bless us to see. Bless us to see that You are The Light that sparked our first germ of life. When You were taking Your time creating us out of love, no one else knew we were there but You.

Our lives started with an intimate moment with our Creator. When we are trying to find Him or believe He exists, we should go back to our moment of creation, when it was only us and Him.

Dear God,

For generations Your women have suffered, sacrificed, survived, endured, fought, fallen, risen, and experienced pain no man could ever sustain mentally or physically. We have been in this wilderness seeking water that only You could provide.

You built us to reproduce You.

You God have suffered, sacrificed, survived, endured, fought, perfected Yourself, experienced pain no man could ever sustain mentally or physically. You have come to this wilderness to save us!

The woman is truly your second self.

As we bow in prayer like the baby in its mothers womb being formed into new life, I ask You to nurture your women. Forgive us of our sin and continue to guide, strengthen and protect us.

Dear God,

Bless my sisters and I to become so strong that nothing can break us. To be healed from all the pain we carry and protected from all of our afflictions. Never make us to be envious or jealous of one another. Let no man come between us.

May our relationships with God grow into our being one with Him! And grow us to see we are His gift to this world. Let us be the example for the world to see what a true woman of God looks like.

Let no one take you off your post.

Walk my sister, in reverence for it is time for our reform.

Dear God,

Free our minds allowing us to be exempt from the captivity of those outside of Your authority. No interference between our communications with You. The only restriction we will feel is our natural compulsion to Your law. Allow us to carry the ability to do all through Your Will.

Bless us to be the trees that produce Your fruit with sincere desires to serve You. Protect us from all that are against us and bless us to be victorious in Your name!

Dear God,

Remove insecurities and labels others have placed on me. Allow me to remain focused on You even when others say I cannot do it. I know I can in Your name.

Guide me so that I don't make mistakes, only learn milestones. I have already fallen, it is time for me to be risen in You. Show the world Your power of the reformation of Your women and lift me to live my greatness which You have destined for me.

Dear God,

I need a moment of Your time. I need Your arms wrapped around me and I need Your merciful ear. I know You have a lot to tend to and I'm sure others are pulling on You. I need this moment to be mine. Just You and me.

God, I need Your healing. I need the scars of my wounds to create scabs of internal healing. Shaping and molding this vessel to present a beautiful image, because right now God, this vessel of Yours is broken and ugly to Your sight. I must have fallen from Your grace, laying on the side of Your deaf ear - the side where Your unfaithful ones dwell.

God, You are my only Father. I need You to take me back. I'm not coming to You like a child, I want to go back to the moment I became Your seed. I want to be replanted in Your soil. I want to be rooted in You, nurtured by You so I may sprout into Your will. I understand the roots of a seed go down before they come back up.

God, I'm already down. I'm in position to receive You. I want to be obedient and faithful like Noah, regardless to what others may say. I want to build Your ark inside of me. I want to embody Your courage like Moses, so I can defeat the Pharaoh of self. I want to devote my entire life to You like Mary who bore Your Jesus, the product of her faith.

Yes, I know, I am more like the Mary of Magdalene. I need You to cleanse me of my demons and allow me to become one of Your best disciples. To become the female to deliver your message so I may witness my own resurrection.

I have faith, I believe in You, and I now sit still, allowing You to restore and replenish my soul.

Dear God,

I'm sorry! I'm sorry for being disobedient and weak. Please grant me the strength to overcome these things. I have previously chosen the wrong way. Allowing the enemy of self to enter my straight path causing me to deviate. And I'm sorry God.

Bless me to fall into Your grace - like a baby in its mother's arms. Encase my heart with Your armor of peace and guide my mind with only Your thoughts. Please, even protect me from the pain my family has caused me.

Bless me God to be convicted in only Your love and I know I won't go wrong again.

Affirming Myself to a New Way of Living

You have to constantly feed yourself positive thoughts, especially if you are in an environment where negativity dwells. If someone is constantly feeding you doubt, words that fuel your insecurities, words that create depression and scars of pain, you have to work double time to deflect that negative energy. You have to prepare your mind for the battlefield you walk through everyday. Establish your heaven in the midst of Satan's hell.

*Experts say that it takes 21 days to **break** a bad habit. It also takes 21 days to **make** a new habit! Our biggest challenge as women is our THINKING. My desire is for you to build the new habit of seeing and affirming yourself in a different way - EVERY DAY!*

Because you have already shown how courageous you are by coming this far in the book, you are ready for your next step.

In the 21-Day Affirmation assignment, you will open your mind to receive a new way of thinking. Take the courageous step to retrain your thoughts by reading the affirmations quietly to yourself a couple of times. The next step is to speak the affirmations into existence – say them out loud!

I am open to receive.
I am ready to change for the better.
I believe in myself.
I deserve this!

I am committed to self-growth.
I am confident I can do this.
I am taking control of my life today!

*I am worth all of the blessings I will receive.
I am strong enough to fight through my trials.
I am endurance.*

*I am equipped to handle the pain that accompanies growth.
I am genetically built to be indestructible.
I am worthy because God blew the breath of life in me!*

I am beautiful.
I am strong.
I am unique.
I am a survivor.
I am a winner.
I overcome difficulties.
I knockout challenges.
I am the best.

I have God-Esteem.

*I give birth to new life.
I am the principles and values of family.
I am sacred.
I am a woman of God.
I am a gift to this world.
I am crowned by God.*

I am the strength of my ancestors!
I am the chant of the slaves.
I am the memory that produces my DNA.

I am the dialect spoken by the original tongue.
I am the energy of the young.
I am the continuation of life!
I am God's spiritual wife.

I am the cartilage mending the backbones that were broken.
I am the cries that died before they were spoken.
I am the beat of the drums that created secret intelligence.
I am the fashion of being, bearing witness to its evidence.

I am produced from the pain hidden in the words of spirituals.
I am a vessel developed out of inspirational; scriptural.

*I am bred out of the sacrifices of soldiers.
I am the wisdom of our elders as they get older.*

*I am not a continent, I am its beginning.
I am not a race or a color; I am the womb that produced its origin.*

I am all that I am because I am a descendent of The ONLY I AM!

I am the peace during time of difficulties.

Become courageous enough to change your surroundings. If you are in an environment or around people who feed you negative energy, who stop you from getting to your next level in life, don't be afraid to let them go. Regardless to whom the person may be. No one is worth your sanity.

You must believe in yourself! You have to stop sacrificing your life for those who live, yet, they leave you dying. Make the decision now to change your reality.

Say to yourself I don't want to live a life of pain anymore. I want to live a better life. I don't want to fall not knowing how to get back up. I don't want to be dropped by others anymore.

I am tired of being broken. Walking around bruised, with a shattered heart, and a confused mind. It is time for me to heal.

I will properly recover from previous experiences that took ownership of my existence and begin living my purpose in life.

I am Greatness.
I am Freedom.
I am Healing.
I am Restored.
I am a New Beginning.
I am Full of Positive Energy.
I am Raised Out of a Fallen State.
I am My Purpose.

I am peaceful.
I am balanced.
I am calm.

I am positive energy.
I am affirmative vibration.
I am relaxed.
I am centered.

I am connected to all that is.
I feed off of my Creator and the Universe.
I am one.

I am in the present moment.
I exist right now.
I am focused.
I am disciplined.

I am in control of my life.

I am inspired.
I am driven.
I am positive motion.
I am a new reality.

I am fearless.
I am courageous.
I am bold.
I am committed.

I am wise.
I am grateful.
I am strength.
I am perseverance.

I am powerful.
I am connected to all that is.

I am living on purpose.
I am successful.
I am valuable.
I am gratitude.

I am love.
I am boundless.
I am creative.
I am confidence.

I am worthy.
I am deserving.
I am good enough.
I am unique.

Release.......

I feel God's energy moving through me.

My mind is reforming. My body is stronger and my soul is at peace.

I release the need to be everyone else but me.
I release the thought that houses negativity.

I release doubt and insecurities.

I release the pain that was placed upon me.
I release the pain that was forced on me.
I release the pain I inherited genetically.

I release the control that others have over me.
I release the darkness that has captivated my sanity.

I release the tears that flow unnaturally.

I am rising into my divinity.
I am exulted in Him who has created me.

My life will shine for eternity.

I am ENOUGH!

God chose me…..

At the moment God chose me, I became free.

Regardless to the color of my skin or the texture of my hair, God chose me.
He took His time and designed what I see.

With love and precision, my actions become His visions.

My trials and my tribulations are His tests that become my testimony,
Because He chose me.

I am strong.
I am natural.
I am unbreakable.

Yet,
I am soft.
I am delicate.
I am unique.

I am courageous.
I am secure.
I am blessed.

*I am grateful.
I am confident.*

I believe in me.

God chose me!

I am a gift to this world.

I am courage.
I am security.
I am blessed.
I am grateful.

I am worthy.
I am faith.
I am confidence.
I am trust.

I am the vessel that extends life.
I am the answer to man's prayers.

I am the key to healing this world's wounds.
I am unconditional love.
I am God's little girl.

I am fun and adventurous.
I laugh.
I smile.
I dance.
I enjoy life.

I illuminate the world.
I shine.
I am God's light!

*I am beautiful.
I respect who I am.
I am confident in myself.
I am natural.*

*I am confortable in my own skin.
I am free of negativity.
I accept how God created me.
I validate myself everyday.*

*I attract positive energy.
I love feeling good about myself.
I believe I am in the image of God.
I have the will power I need!
My inner light is connected to God's Light!*

I am a praying woman.
I am one with God and God is one with me.
God is around me and He protects me.
I believe in the unseen.

God's power is limitless.
I am in His image carrying the power to overcome all things.

My prayers are delivered and heard.
My prayers are answered.
I am an open vessel ready to receive and do God's will.

*I am faith,
I can rise above my fears,
I am faith,
I accept the cleansing process provided by my tears,*

*My faith increases with every breath He gives me,
My faith is attached to God's Will that sets me free,
I am the faith submitting obediently,*

*I am faith larger than the size of a mustard seed,
I am faith walking- allowing the captive slave inside to be freed,*

*I am the faith that bears its own cross working off its sins,
I am faith in God born again!*

I will surround myself with positive energy.
I will surround myself with like minds.

I will change my thoughts that I have the ability to change.
I will change my environment to represent where I desire to be in life.

I will only eat foods that nurture my being.
I will only feed my mind what produces growth and prosperity.

I will feed my inner self peace and harmony, matching my outer well-being.
I will feed on God's Love making it impossible for others to hurt me.

I will allow God's Truth to heal me.

Now be sure to feed your mind positive thoughts everyday starting when you wake up in the morning. Make a list of positive thoughts you know you need to start feeding yourself right away. You can even research affirmations online so that you can create positive thoughts you may not have thought of on your own.

Welcome to your rebirth of a constant, positive energy flow!

Goal Setting

Setting goals is a way to get control of your life. You want them to be precise, measurable, attainable, relevant and time based. You need a goal that is clear with a comprehensible way to obtain it.

Create a list of goals you want to accomplish over the next six months. No more than five goals. These goals have to be in the category of self-love, happiness, surrounding yourself with positive people, appreciation and giving back.

Place the most difficult goal in the middle and establish easy targets/action items to accomplish this goal. Once you have listed your five goals, state the timeframe it will take to accomplish the goal. In this process, you don't want to underestimate your ability to complete a task quickly and you don't want to overwhelm yourself with too much. Be realistic in your timeframes and remember to stay focused so you hit the goal!

All of your goals should have listed with them a set of targets leading up to the actual goal. It is important to see immediate wins along the way. It validates your ability to reach your targets.

When you have completed a target you will build self-esteem, confidence, and faith that you can reach the goal. Make sure the goals you set are for you! Not to please other people, but to please yourself. Do not concern yourself with what other people think. Your goals are to improve you! You may come across people who don't agree with your goals. You must keep in mind that what others think does not matter. What matters is that you are taking the time to create a better you.

Goal	Short Term/Long Term	I Will/Action Steps	Time Frame	Completed

Acknowledgements

I thank God for blessing me with life. I am forever grateful!

The words in this book could not have been written if God did not bless my life to be carried in the vessel of my mother. Both my mother and my paternal grandmother are the examples who have lived many of the words written in this book. I am forever grateful for them both.

I thank Allah (God) for The Teachings of The Most Honorable Elijah Muhammad and the living example of those teachings, The Honorable Minister Louis Farrakhan. If I had not come into those teachings, this book would not have been possible.

I thank The Honorable Minister Louis Farrakhan for the beautiful words he has spoken to me that nurtured the seed God had placed in me. He gave me light in my time of darkness. He gave me peace in the midst of confusion. I thank Allah for him and his dedication to the upliftment of our people.

I thank my husband for assisting with the graphic designs of the cover of this book, but most of all I thank him for his patience and standing by me, helping my dream manifest.

I thank the beautiful women God blessed me to gain sisterhood with, who truly believed in me even in moments that I didn't believe in myself. They pushed me and inspired me to do God's work even when I felt like I wasn't deserving of this work. They were the reminder that I am. Those beautiful women are Sis. Akilah Muhammad, Sis. Mareshah Muhammad, Sis. Rachel X and Sis. Leah Muhammad.

I thank the girls who were eager to be apart of the "I Am Enough" project. Those girls are Nasira Muhammad, Kenya Muhammad, Aminah Hakim, Aamirah Wells, Nurrah Muhammad, Mahasin Muhammad, Ruqaya Muhammad, Nyah Tsai, Londyn Woods, Madinah Muhammad, Alimmah Muhammad, Ahmadiyyah Muhammad, Khadijah Muhammad, and Jameelah Taylor.

I thank my editors for taking the time out of their busy schedules to edit this book, Sis. Akilah, Sis. Mareshah, Sis. Nasira Muhammad and Sis. Ameenah Kelly.

I thank the beautiful women whose pictures you see on the cover of this book. Sis. Nasira Muhammad, Sis.

Jamillah Farrakhan, Jada Cannon, Aamirah Wells, Sis. Khadijah Muhammad, Sis. Nurrah Muhammad and Sis. Aneesa Muhammad.

www.ingramcontent.com/pod-product-compliance
Lightning Source LLC
Chambersburg PA
CBHW072038110526
44592CB00012B/1466